I0605415

THE SECRETS OF MUSHROOMS

ILLUSTRATIONS BY
ESTER CASTELNUOVO
AND VALENTINA FIGUS

TEXT BY
GINEVRA PICOCO
AND LORENZO COCCHI

CONTENTS

There is a whole natural world around us where a huge amount of life flourishes. It's so big that it's almost impossible to imagine.

Most of us know a lot about plants and animals, but we usually can't say the same about mushrooms. Their world is immense and mysterious – it surrounds us, but is hidden from view.

So, get ready to set off on an unforgettable journey to discover the incredible and brightly colored kingdom of mushrooms!

This book will teach you all about the life of mushrooms: how they are born, how they grow and how they reproduce. You will discover their incredible habits and friendships . . . Sometimes they are truly unbelievable!

HOW MUSHROOMS EVOLVED

The history of mushrooms dates back **millions of years** and is based on links with other organisms, including **us animals**. The most ancient ancestors of mushrooms were **microscopic**; they lived in the seas and, most likely, were **parasites** of other organisms.

THE EARTH'S FIRST MUSHROOMS

The first mushrooms made their way out of the water thanks to an extraordinary alliance with the first **earthly algae**. The land that emerged was a very harsh place, so to be able to settle there they needed to join forces in symbiosis (more on this in Chapter 3).

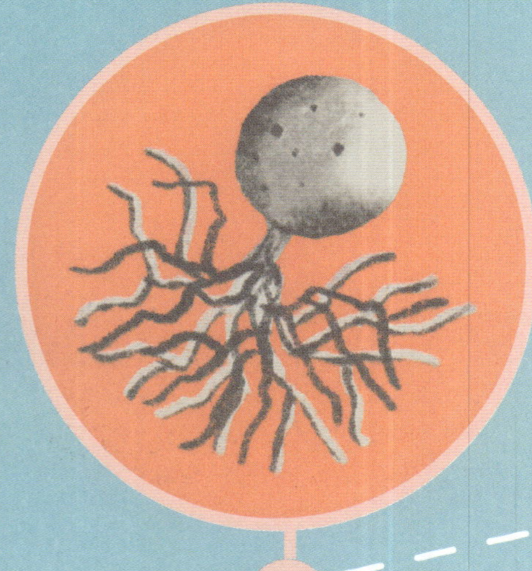

LICHENS AND GIANT MUSHROOMS

A new symbiosis between fungi and algae, the **lichen**, began to spread quickly: it is an alliance that has lasted to this day!

You could also have found **giant mushrooms**, up to 26 feet tall and able to shade most of the plants around them, which were still quite short.

They were among the masters of the Earth!

THE RELATIONSHIP WITH PLANTS

Giant mushrooms became extinct, and **plants** grew taller thanks to **wood**: a new material that allowed them to get stronger.

By staying close to the plants, mushrooms were able to benefit from their success and also thrived.

650

450

350

MILLION YEARS AGO

"SCAVENGER" MUSHROOMS

The largest **extinction** that has ever struck our planet destroyed most life-forms. The **decomposer mushrooms** feeding on dead organic matter found themselves surrounded by a world full of food in which they triumphed.

THE TURN OF ASCOMYCETES AND BASIDIOMYCETES

Mushrooms coexisted with **dinosaurs** for thousands of years. The **extinction** that happened **65 million years ago** made these gigantic animals disappear and spared only a few lucky groups of living beings, including many **mushrooms**. These, once again, managed to benefit from the disaster and, by recycling all the available organic material, laid the foundations for new life.

Without their work we probably wouldn't exist today.

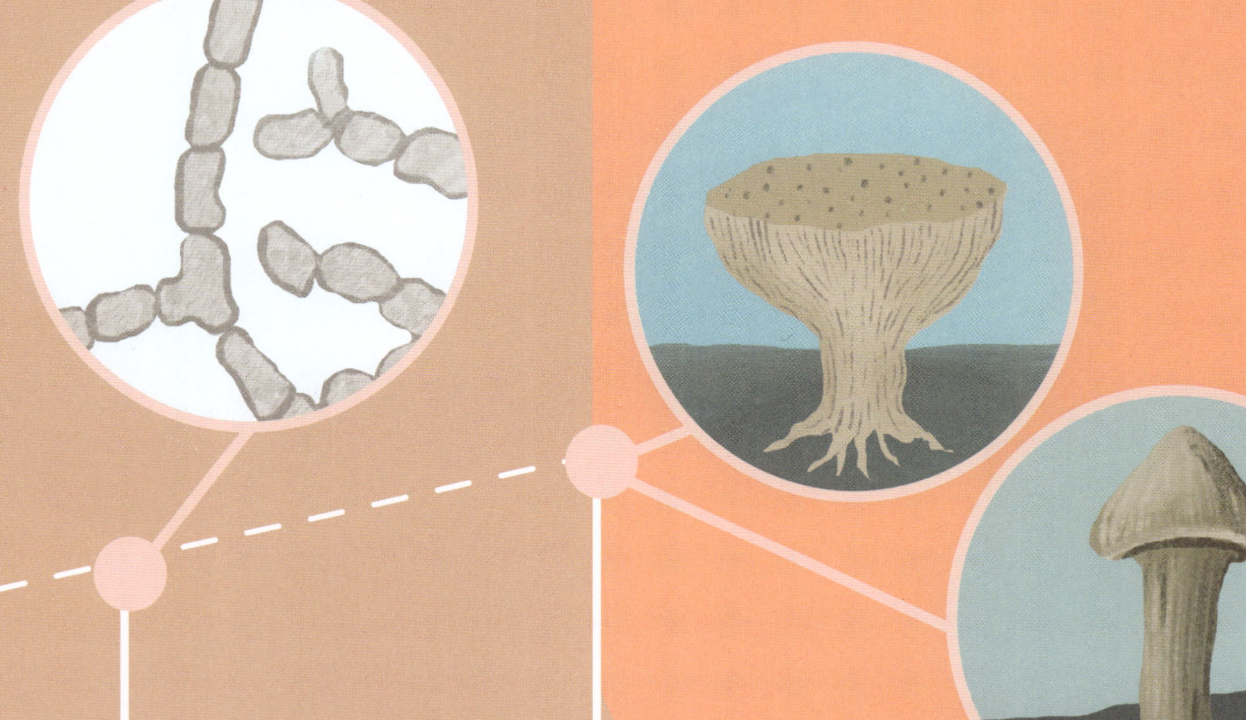

250

65

MILLION YEARS AGO

SO, WHO OR WHAT ARE MUSHROOMS?

There are around 150,000 species of mushrooms known today. That may seem a lot, but in reality, they represent only a tiny part of those thought to exist on Earth.

THERE MAY IN FACT BE OVER 3 MILLION SPECIES OF MUSHROOMS, MOST STILL WAITING TO BE DISCOVERED!

Mushrooms are truly bizarre *eukaryotic* organisms: they have characteristics common to both plants and animals but they form a kingdom of their own!

PAST MISTAKES

Since they don't move and their cells are similar to those of plants, for centuries mushrooms were considered strange primitive plant organisms!

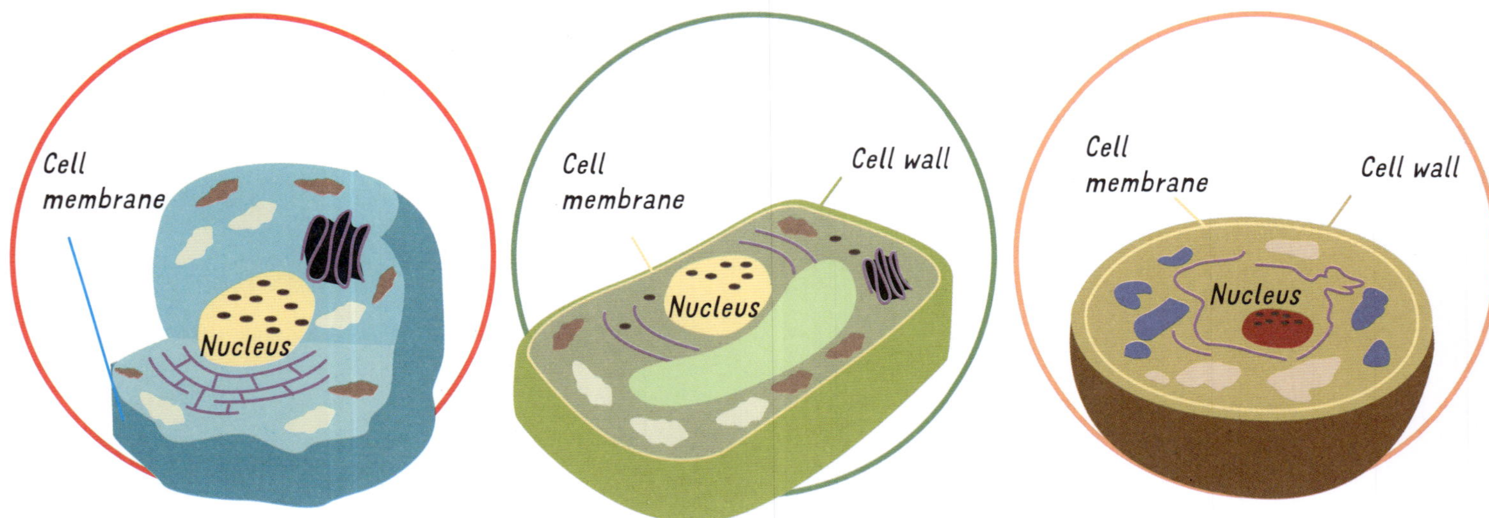

MORE PLANT OR MORE ANIMAL?

Although they appear so different, mushrooms actually have more in common with us animals than with plants. Like animals, mushrooms are *heterotrophic* organisms and, although they have a cell wall, like plants, this is not made of cellulose but of *chitin* — a substance found in the shells of insects and crustaceans.

IN SHORT . . . THEY REALLY SEEM TO BE AN EVOLUTIONARY MIX!

EUKARYOTES: organisms made up of cells with a nucleus.

ETHEROTROPHS: organisms that get their food and energy from substances produced by other living beings.

CHITIN: the main substance that makes up the exoskeleton (shell) of arthropods (insects, arachnids, crustaceans).

THE LIVING ORGANISMS OF OUR PLANET

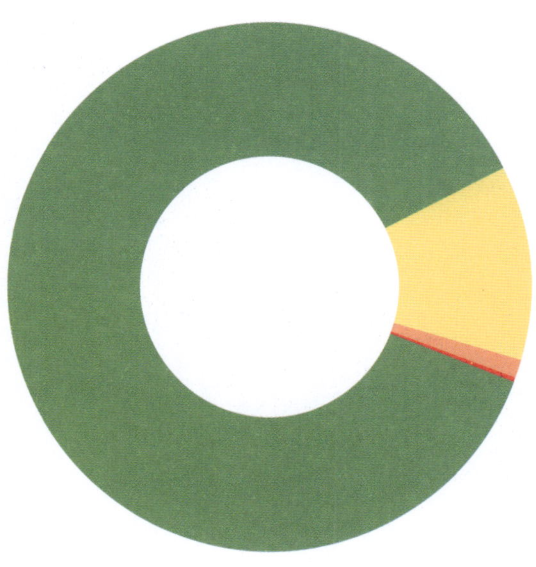

In first place are **PLANTS**, which clearly make up the majority of living beings on our planet.

Then we find **MICROORGANISMS**: living beings so small that they cannot be seen with the naked eye.

MUSHROOMS are in third place and add up to four times the number of all animals (including us humans)—and that's just the ones we know about!

This tiny red portion represents all the **ANIMALS** on our planet (from midges to whales and humans).

THE FIVE MAIN GROUPS OF THE MUSHROOM KINGDOM HAVE NAMES THAT ARE AS BIZARRE AS THEY LOOK!

Their name always ends with "mycete", which means . . . "mushroom".

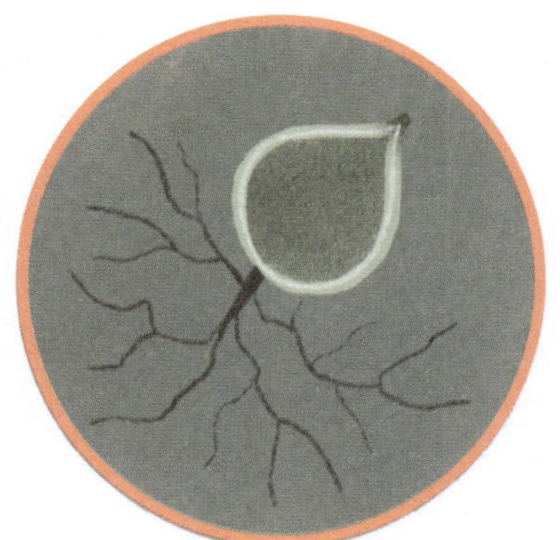

▪ CHYTRIDIOMYCETES
Over 1,000 known species.
Microscopic and usually aquatic fungi; parasites of algae, mushrooms, or animals.

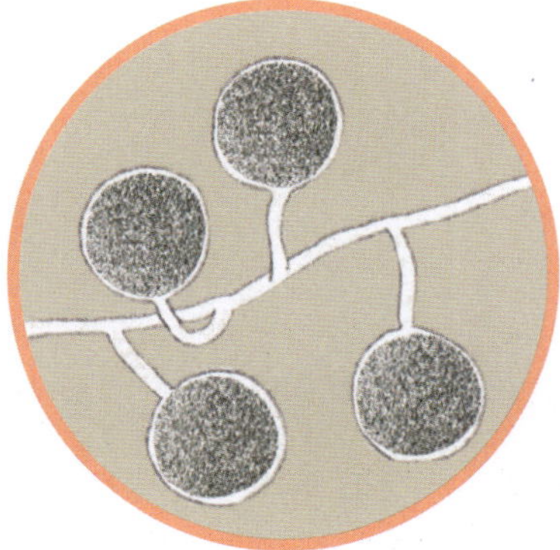

▪ GLOMEROMYCETES
About 300 known species.
Underground fungi that live in symbiosis with plant roots.

▪ MUCOROMYCETES
About 350 known species.
Molds, such as those that grow on bread, fruit, and vegetables.

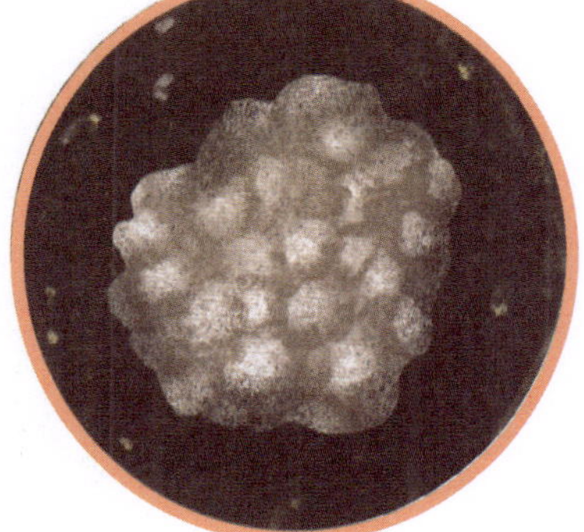

▪ ASCOMYCETES
More than 30,000 known species.
Molds, yeasts, truffles, lichens, and more.

▪ BASIDIOMYCETES
More than 30,000 known species.
Mushrooms with the typical umbrella appearance.

MUSHROOMS ALL AROUND THE WORLD

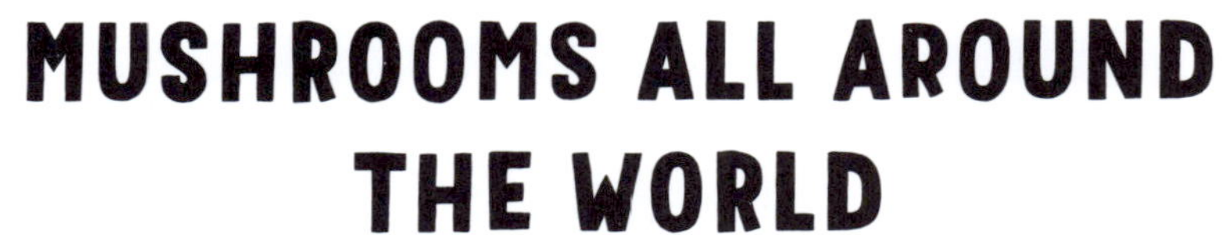

**EVERY CORNER OF OUR PLANET,
EVEN THE MOST UNIMAGINABLE AND HARSH,
IS INHABITED BY MUSHROOMS!**

▪ **DESERTS**
Water is essential for mushrooms but **some mushrooms are able to survive among the desert sands**, an environment that seems too dry for the life of any organism.

▪ **POLAR REGIONS**
Although the low temperatures and limited food available make these places very unwelcoming, **some mushrooms do grow among frozen lands and sharp rocks.**

▪ THE FOREST

Whether we are talking about temperate or tropical forests, mushrooms love to grow in environments that are rich in nutrients and plants. **This climate is often helpful for their development.**

SOME MUSHROOMS HAVE EVEN BEEN SENT INTO SPACE SO WE CAN STUDY THEIR EXTRAORDINARY RESILIENCE!

▪ CITIES

Mushrooms concrete and bricks! They peep out in gardens, flower beds, and flowerpots on our balconies. **Every now and then they are so strong that they even pop up from the asphalt or the walls of old houses.**

▪ HUMAN BEINGS AND ANIMALS

Some fungi also live inside the **bodies of animals**. Humans don't usually find them very dangerous, but for many plants and insects they can be deadly!

CHAPTER 1

WHAT MUSHROOMS LOOK LIKE

What are those strange little umbrellas peeking out from the woodland floor?

What we see poking out from the ground are the fruits of mushrooms: the sporophores.

BUT ARE YOU SURE THERE IS NOTHING UNDERNEATH?

THE MUSHROOMS AROUND US

Snuggled surrounded by the roots of plants, among fallen leaves, inside the trunks of trees, or under their bark, real mushrooms extend invisibly all around us in the form of tiny filaments, the **mycelium**.

THE MYCELIUM AND THE HYPHAE

The **mycelium** is made up of many small cells joined together; they are called **hyphae**.

ALL PARTS OF THE MUSHROOM ARE MADE OF MYCELIUM, INCLUDING THE DENSE WEB HIDDEN FROM VIEW AND ITS WONDERFUL FRUITS, THE SPOROPHORES.

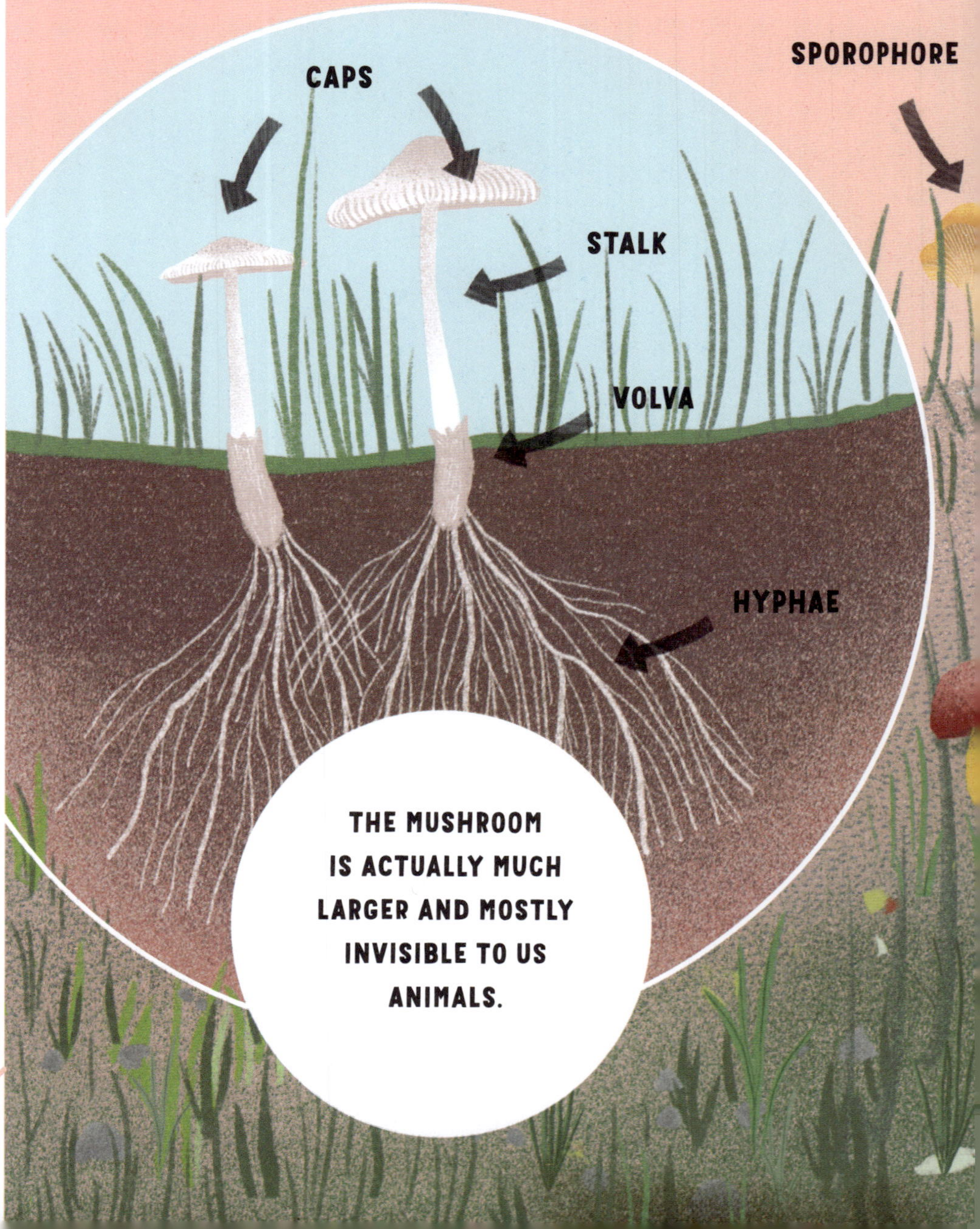

CAPS
SPOROPHORE
STALK
VOLVA
HYPHAE

THE MUSHROOM IS ACTUALLY MUCH LARGER AND MOSTLY INVISIBLE TO US ANIMALS.

▪ THE FOREST

Whether we are talking about temperate or tropical forests, mushrooms love to grow in environments that are rich in nutrients and plants. **This climate is often helpful for their development.**

SOME MUSHROOMS HAVE EVEN BEEN SENT INTO SPACE SO WE CAN STUDY THEIR EXTRAORDINARY RESILIENCE!

▪ CITIES

Mushrooms concrete and bricks! They peep out in gardens, flower beds, and flowerpots on our balconies. **Every now and then they are so strong that they even pop up from the asphalt or the walls of old houses.**

▪ HUMAN BEINGS AND ANIMALS

Some fungi also live inside the **bodies of animals**. Humans don't usually find them very dangerous, but for many plants and insects they can be deadly!

CHAPTER 1

WHAT MUSHROOMS LOOK LIKE

What are those strange little umbrellas peeking out from the woodland floor?

What we see poking out from the ground are the fruits of mushrooms: the sporophores.

BUT ARE YOU SURE THERE IS NOTHING UNDERNEATH?

THE MUSHROOMS AROUND US

Snuggled surrounded by the roots of plants, among fallen leaves, inside the trunks of trees, or under their bark, real mushrooms extend invisibly all around us in the form of tiny filaments, the **mycelium**.

THE MYCELIUM AND THE HYPHAE

The **mycelium** is made up of many small cells joined together; they are called **hyphae**.

ALL PARTS OF THE MUSHROOM ARE MADE OF MYCELIUM, INCLUDING THE DENSE WEB HIDDEN FROM VIEW AND ITS WONDERFUL FRUITS, THE SPOROPHORES.

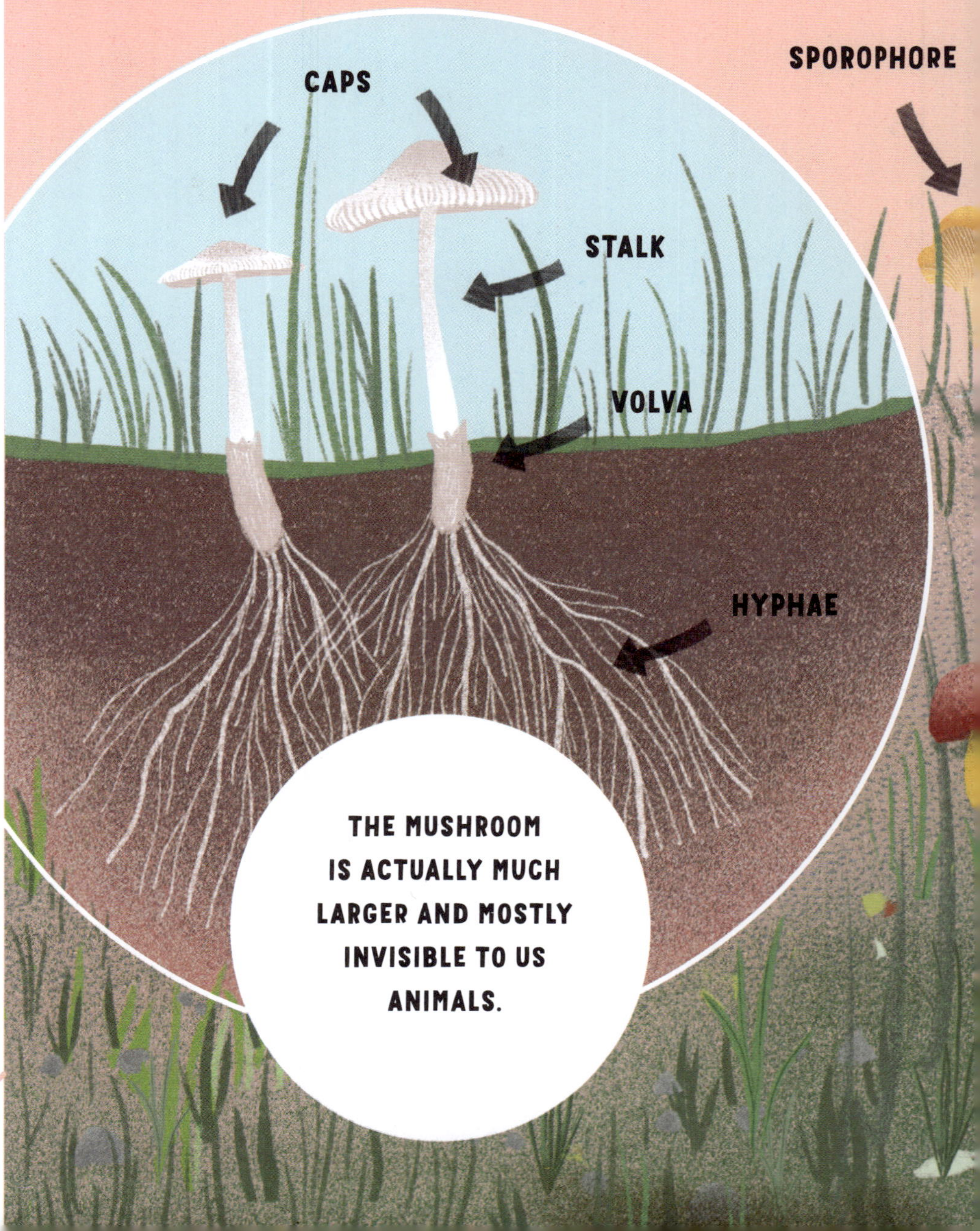

CAPS

SPOROPHORE

STALK

VOLVA

HYPHAE

THE MUSHROOM IS ACTUALLY MUCH LARGER AND MOSTLY INVISIBLE TO US ANIMALS.

BUT . . . IS THAT ALL?

Mushrooms are much larger than the **fruits** that they produce. They use their hidden part to protect themselves, explore, spread out, find food, and form relationships with other living beings. The visible part, the **sporophore**, allows them to scatter and reproduce.

THE SPOROPHORE

There are incredible differences between mushroom species, but even the same mushroom changes shape as it grows. At the right time, the **underground mycelium** begins to produce one or more of its "fruits"—**the sporophores**—that, starting from small **buds**, grow and grow until they look like what we usually call **mushrooms**. In the initial stages of this process, many mushrooms have **veils** that cover them, either partly or fully. As they grow, these veils break, leaving very pretty decorations on the **cap** and **stalk**.

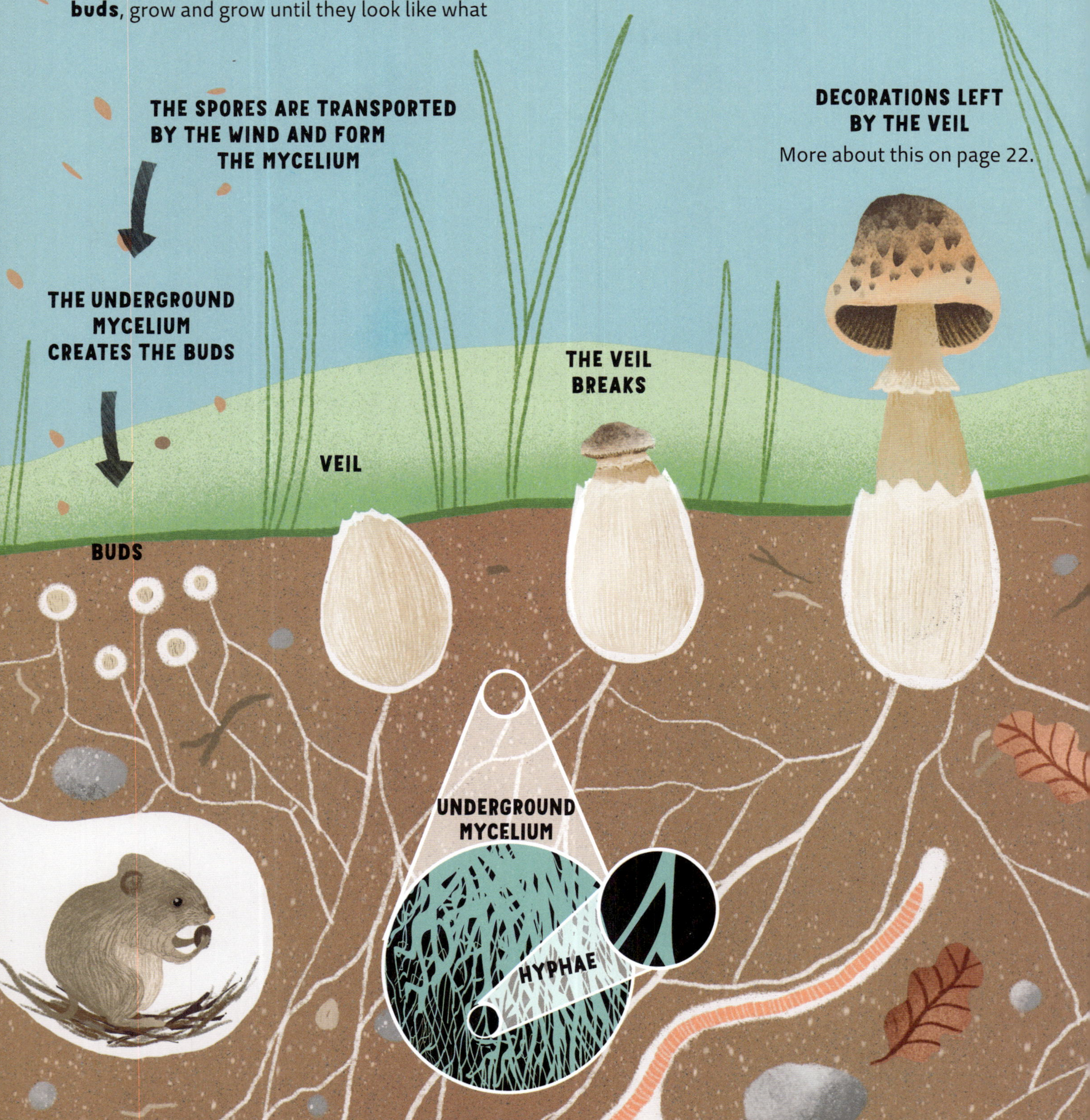

THE PARTS OF THE SPOROPHORE

The **cap** is the upper part of the mushroom, attached to the **stalk**. It is covered by the **cuticle**.

CAP

PRODUCTIVE MYCELIUM

CUTICLE

The **cuticle** is a thin "skin"; it can be plain or have spectacular decorations.

RING

The **ring** is an elegant structure that decorates the **stalk**.

HYMENOPHORE

The **hymenophore** is the lower part of the cap, where the spores are produced.

STALK

The **stalk** holds up the **cap**. Both can be plain or decorated.

TURN THE PAGE TO FIND OUT MORE ABOUT SPOROPHORES AND THEIR PARTS.

SHAPES OF THE SPOROPHORE

Not all mushroom sporophores have the classic umbrella shape. Prepare to be amazed!

A MUSHROOM'S APPEARANCE MAY BE SURPRISING, OR SO STRANGE THAT IT DOESN'T EVEN LOOK LIKE A MUSHROOM.

Morchella esculenta

It is easy to understand why they are called "sponges"...

THEIR CAPS LOOK JUST LIKE A SPONGE!

Calocera viscosa

A yellow flame in the woodland!

THEY REACH OUT TO THE SKY AND ARE VERY DISTINCTIVE.

Clathrus ruber

Also known as the "lantern mushroom", this sporophore grows by hatching out of a kind of egg.

ONCE FULLY GROWN, IT TURNS BRIGHT RED AND GIVES OUT A TERRIBLE SMELL TO ATTRACT INSECTS!

Hydnellum peckii

Strange and brightly colored.

THE SPOROPHORES OF THIS MUSHROOM STICK OUT OF THE WOODLAND FLOOR LIKE HUGE TEETH COVERED WITH TINY BLOOD-RED DROPS!

Hericium erinaceus

A tree with a beard?

NOT QUITE! THIS UNIQUE MUSHROOM DECORATES THE TRUNKS OF TREES AND, CLOSE UP, LOOKS LIKE THE STALACTITES FOUND IN CAVES.

Astraeus hygrometricus

The name is no coincidence: this mushroom helps us to measure humidity, just like a hygrometer does!

WHEN IT IS HUMID, THE “STAR” OPENS AND RELEASES THE SPORES.

THE CAP

The cap is the part of the **sporophore** found at the top of the **stalk** and it is usually covered by the **cuticle** (a thin "skin"). Under the **cap** is the **hymenophore,** where the **spores** are produced.

THE FIRST THING THAT YOU NOTICE IS ITS SHAPE.

There are lots of caps of different colors, sizes, and shapes, even between mushrooms of the same species.

SHAPE
The shape of a cap changes as it grows. Initially, it is **folded up**, but then it opens more and more, like an umbrella.

EDGE (BORDER)
Can be flat, folded downward, folded upward, serrated, hairy, etc.

CUTICLE
Can be smooth, rough, dry, or slimy and it may have fantastic decorations like verrucae, scales, etc.

HYMENOPHORE
The part that produces the spores. Again, there is an incredible variety of shapes: gills, tubules and pores, spikes, etc.

DISCOVER THE NAMES OF THESE MUSHROOMS, ACCORDING TO THE SHAPE OF THEIR CAP.

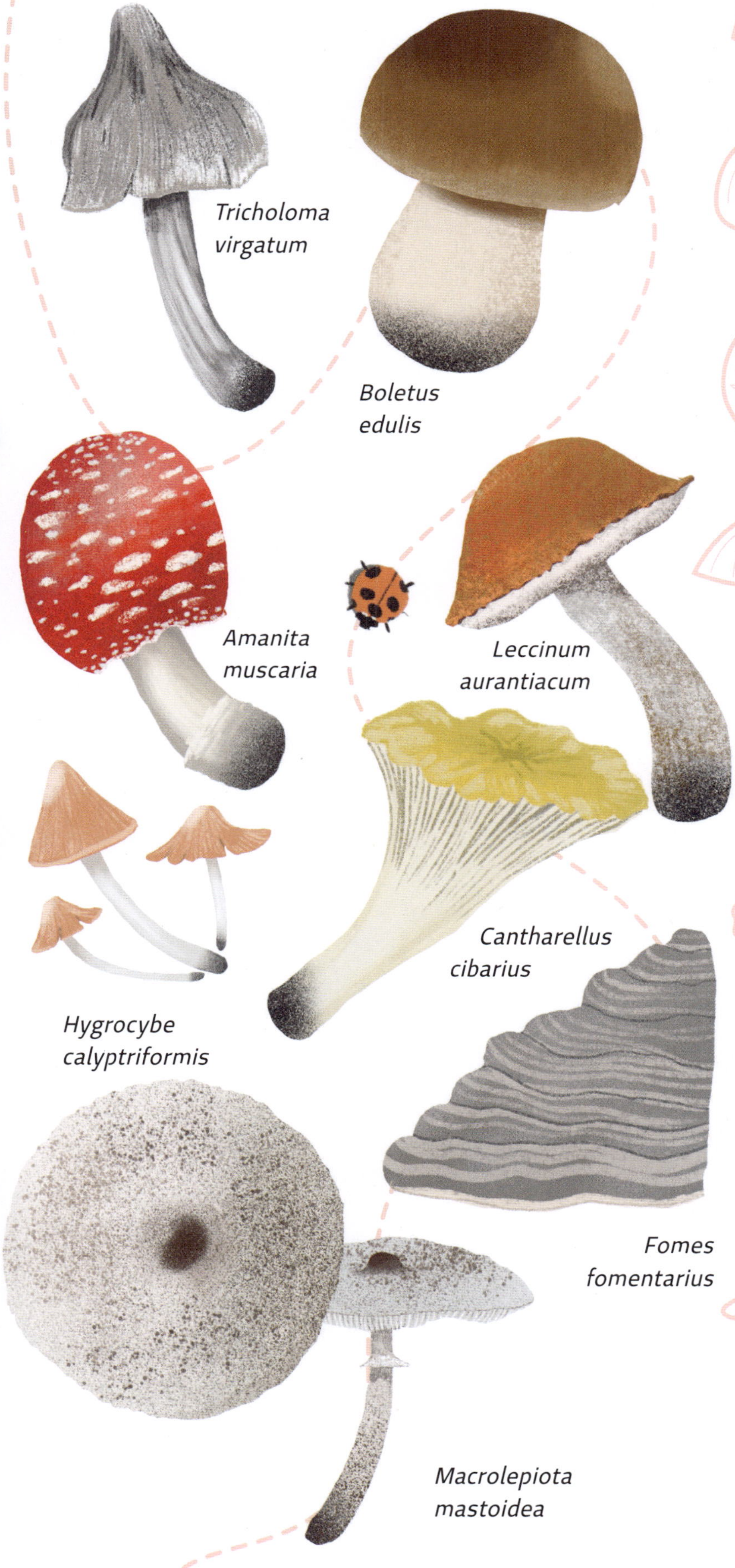

Tricholoma virgatum

Boletus edulis

Amanita muscaria

Leccinum aurantiacum

Cantharellus cibarius

Hygrocybe calyptriformis

Fomes fomentarius

Macrolepiota mastoidea

THE SHAPE OF CAPS

▪ **BELL-SHAPED:**
these look like a bell and can vary in height and size.

▪ **HEMISPHERIC:**
in the shape of a half-sphere.

▪ **GLOBE:**
in the shape of a sphere, folded in on itself until it touches the stalk.

▪ **CONVEX:**
slightly more fuller than a half-sphere, but not quite flat.

▪ **CONICAL:**
in the shape of a cone, and usually slim, depending on the species.

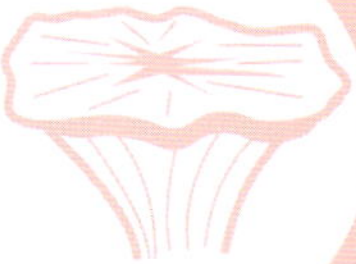

▪ **FUNNEL-SHAPE:**
they look like a funnel!

▪ **SHELF-SHAPE:**
like shelves but made out of mycelium!

▪ **CYMBAL-SHAPED:**
with a raised "button" in the middle, like a cymbal.

ONE SINGLE MUSHROOM CAN TAKE ON DIFFERENT SHAPES AS IT GROWS.

NOW YOU TRY!

Try to find all the mushrooms that you have been reading about.

Their names are below, but don't worry if you can't remember what all of them look like: you can go back to check the previous pages!

Tricholoma virgatum ▪ *Leccinum aurantiacum* ▪ *Boletus edulis* ▪ *Cantharellus cibarius* ▪ *Macrolepiota mastoidea* ▪ *Hygrocybe calyptriformis* ▪ *Fomes fomentarius* ▪ *Amanita muscaria*

THE VEILS

The veils are layers that protect the **sporophore** during the first phases of its growth.

There are two different types of veils: the general veil and the partial veil.

The general veil completely covers the entire sporophore, a bit like an eggshell.

CHARACTERISTICS
The general veil breaks when the sporophore starts growing.

AS THE VEIL BREAKS, IT LEAVES TRACES THAT LOOK LIKE BEAUTIFUL DECORATIONS ON THE CAP AND AT THE BASE OF THE STALK.

Not all mushrooms have veils.

WHAT'S LEFT ON THE CUTICLE
These are small pieces in all shapes and colors, left by the breaking of the general veil, which decorate the cuticle of all mushrooms.

VOLVA
This is the structure found at the base of the stalk: it can be very strong and look like a bag, or fragile and look like small verrucae or scales.

THE PARTIAL VEIL ONLY PROTECTS THE PART WHERE THE SPORES GROW (HYMENOPHORE)

CHARACTERISTICS

The partial veil **breaks** when the fully grown **spores** need to scatter and no longer need to be protected.

THE BREAKING OF THE PARTIAL VEIL MAY ALSO LEAVE TELLTALE TRACES, SUCH AS RINGS, CURTAINS, AND DECORATIONS ON THE EDGE OF THE CAP.

WHAT'S LEFT ON THE EDGE OF THE CAP?

Different pieces left by the breaking of the partial veil decorate the **edge of the cap** on some mushrooms.

RING

The ring is a spectacular structure that surrounds and decorates the stalk of some mushrooms. Usually, it is what's left of the partial veil but, in some cases, it can be what remains of the general veil.

THE STALK

The stalk is the part of the mushroom that holds the cap. It is not always tall or slim and, sometimes, it is even completely missing, as in shelf mushrooms.

IT MAY SEEM RATHER PLAIN BUT IF YOU LOOK AT IT CAREFULLY, THE STALK HAS CHARACTERISTICS THAT MAKE IT STAND OUT!

SHAPE OF THE STALK

Round or thin, similar to a club or a pear, slim or squat: these are the many shapes that make each mushroom unique.

AND WHAT'S IT LIKE INSIDE?

Even the inside of a mushroom can be surprising: sometimes full and compact; other times it is hollow like a straw or full of mycelium, with a squishy texture.

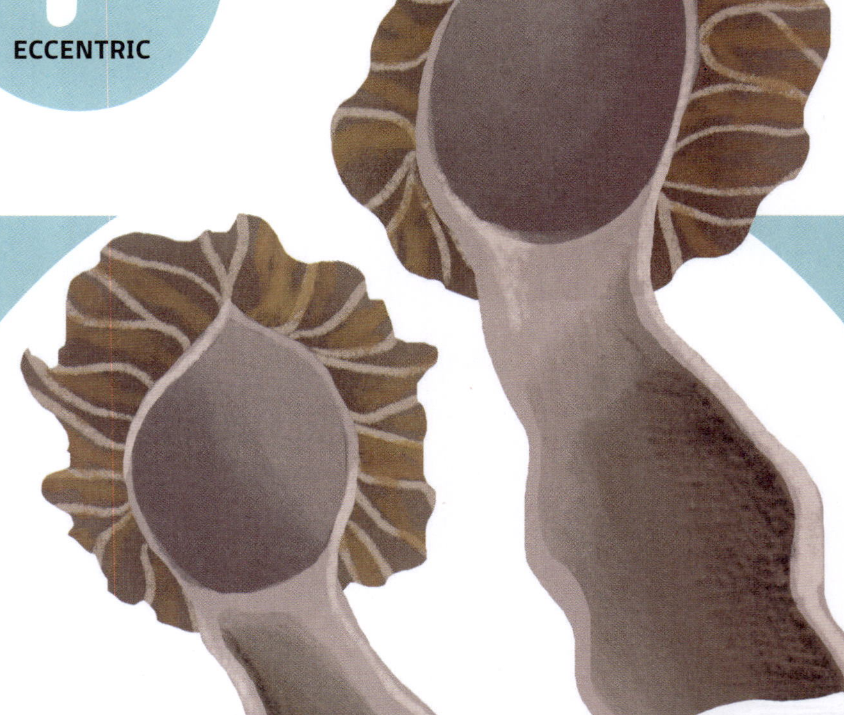

DECORATIONS
Similar to those found on the cap, the stalk may have **beautiful decorations,** such as small dimples, dots, crisscrosses, spots, and patterns that look like mosaics—true works of art.

SURFACE
Smooth or wrinkled, spotty or web-like; a mushroom's surface can be dry, slimy, wet or even greasy!

FLESH
The stalk can have a firm, hard consistency; it can be stringy like celery stalks, or it can be weak and delicate.

IT'S BEST NOT TO TASTE IT!

It is important to remember never to eat any mushrooms found in the wild, as they may be toxic. When trying to recognize them, you need to use your other senses.

Never eat a mushroom that hasn't been checked by an expert!

SMELL

Some mushrooms have a yummy smell similar to, for example, garlic, orange, honey, licorice, flour, cheese, cocoa . . . It's almost like being in the kitchen!

Others smell very strange: glue, paint, soap, disinfectant, rubber.

Some even smell like sweat, rotten meat, and poo. Yuck!

WARNING! A GOOD SMELL DOES NOT ALWAYS MEAN THE MUSHROOM IS EDIBLE: THERE ARE MANY TOXIC SPECIES THAT SMELL DELICIOUS!

HEARING

Our hearing is not particularly useful in the study of mushrooms, but it can come in handy every now and then.

The stalk of an important family of mushrooms (*russulaceae*) makes a distinctive "**tock**!" sound when broken, like the sound of a piece of **chalk** being snapped in two.

TOUCH

Touching mushrooms can tell us a lot about how they are made: some are as hard as wood, while others are so elastic that they snap back to their original shape after being bent. And others are soft, gelatinous, and slimy. Some mushrooms are smooth or velvety to the touch; others are wrinkled, rough, or even hairy.

SIGHT

We can see mushrooms that are bright or light, matte or shiny, and mushrooms of all different shapes and sizes.

THE APPEARANCE OF MUSHROOMS IS SUPER FASCINATING, BUT BE CAREFUL: THE SAME SPECIES OF MUSHROOM CAN APPEAR IN DIFFERENT SHAPES, COLORS, AND SIZES - SIGHT IS NOT ENOUGH TO UNDERSTAND WHAT IS IN FRONT OF US!

Sight can give us a great show when we encounter bioluminescent mushrooms! Turn the page to find out more.

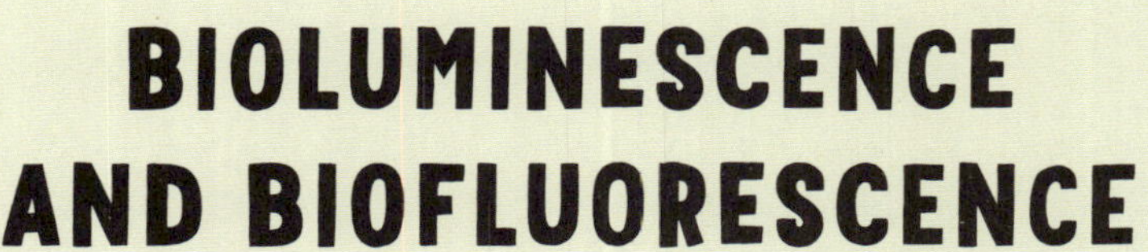

BIOLUMINESCENCE AND BIOFLUORESCENCE

When the sun sets, it doesn't just go dark for the night: many living beings make themselves known under the cover of darkness!

Those that shine with their own light, like fireflies, are called bioluminescent and always produce a greenish glow, which is the result of chemical reactions within the body. However, there are **BIOFLUORESCENT MUSHROOMS** that shine brightly when hit by **ULTRAVIOLET** light. In this case the luminescence is not produced by the fungus but caused by the light beam.

MANY SCIENTISTS NOW THINK THAT THE **BIOLUMINESCENCE** ATTRACTS NOCTURNAL INSECTS. THEY CAN'T RESIST THE GLOW OF THE **LAMP-MUSHROOM**, AND SO END UP SCATTERING THE SPORES THAT GOT STUCK TO THEM WHILE VISITING THE MUSHROOM.

Omphalotus olearius

Panellus stipticus

We still know very little about biofluorescence: it is very difficult to study and explain.
BIOLUMINESCENT MUSHROOMS ONLY SHINE IN VARIOUS SHADES OF GREEN, WHEREAS **BIOFLUORESCENT** ONES SHINE WITH ANY COLORS, AS LONG AS THEY ARE LIT BY A SOURCE OF **ULTRAVIOLET LIGHT**.
Leratiomyces squamosus
BIOFLUORESCENCE
WE OFTEN DISCOVER BIOFLURESCENCE IN SPECIES THAT WE ARE ALREADY FAMILIAR WITH, BUT WHICH WE HAVE NEVER SEEN IN THE RIGHT LIGHT.
Panellus stipticus

RECORD-BREAKING MUSHROOMS!

Mushrooms amaze us with their variety of shapes, colors, and adaptations, but the **records** they hold are even more mind-boggling!

THE OLDEST MUSHROOM

Phellinus ellipsoideus

Fossil strands and mycelium-like structures have been discovered in the Democratic Republic of the Congo, within very ancient rocks.

ANALYSIS HAS SHOWN THAT THESE FOSSIL REMAINS DATE BACK TO ABOUT 800 MILLION YEARS AGO!

Armillaria ostoyae

Its mycelium extends for miles in the Malheur Forest in the USA.

CONSIDERED ONE OF THE LARGEST ORGANISMS IN THE WORLD, ITS FAR LARGER THAN THE BLUE WHALE.

THE BIGGEST MUSHROOM

IT OCCUPIES MORE THAN 2,000 ACRES—THE SAME AS ABOUT 1,350 SOCCER FIELDS!

Ophiocordyceps sinensis and *Tuber magnatum*

One kilogram of *Ophiocordyceps sinensis* as well as the same amount of *Tuber magnatum*, the renowned **white truffle**, were sold for the incredible price of around €100,000.

THERE ARE MUSHROOMS SO PRESTIGIOUS THAT THEY ARE WORTH A FORTUNE!

Gibberella zeae

Really tiny fungal cannons: it has been calculated that the mushroom *Gibberella zeae* releases its **spore** with an incredible speed equal to 870,000 times the force of gravity.

IT'S AS IF A SMALL FUNGAL SPORE COULD OVERTAKE A POWERFUL SPACE ROCKET AT FULL SPEED!

TURN THE PAGE TO FIND OUT ABOUT POISONOUS MUSHROOMS.

Phellinus ellipsoideus

It is 33 feet long , over 3 feet wide, and 2 inches deep! This **polypore** originates on the island of Hainan, in southern China, and is particularly fond of trees.

THANKS TO ITS HUGE SIZE AND WEIGHT, IT HAS WON THE TITLE OF MUSHROOM WITH THE LARGEST SPOROPHORE EVER REPORTED.

MORE THAN 1,000 POUNDS!

THE LARGEST SPOROPHORE

MUSHROOMS TO AVOID!

Mushrooms are really easy to mistake, and this often makes it difficult to be sure what we are dealing with. Many of them contain **toxins**: substances that can be harmful to us or are even deadly. It is therefore extremely **dangerous** to eat mushrooms when you are not completely certain what they are.

THERE ARE ALSO MANY THOERIES ABOUT MUSHROOMS AND THEIR TOXICITY. HERE ARE THE SILLIEST . . .

Mushrooms eaten by animals are edible.

FALSE! SNAILS AND SLUGS ARE FOND OF A NUMBER OF DEADLY MUSHROOMS.

Lepiota cristata

Amanita phalloides

Lepiota aspera

Mushrooms that smell nice are edible.

FALSE! THERE ARE SOME TOXIC MUSHROOMS THAT PRODUCE A LIGHT, PLEASANT, FRUITY ODOUR.

Mushrooms that have a sweet taste are edible.

FALSE!
SOME DEADLY MUSHROOMS HAVE A SWEET TASTE!

THE ONLY WAY TO KNOW WHETHER A MUSHROOM IS TOXIC OR EDIBLE IS BY RECOGNIZING WHICH SPECIES IT BELONGS TO, AND THAT'S NOT EASY AT ALL.

THIS IS WHY MYCOLOGISTS EXIST; THEY ARE MUSHROOM EXPERTS AND KNOW WHAT TO LOOK OUT FOR!

An edible mushroom growing near a toxic one becomes just as toxic.

FALSE!
MUSHROOMS DO NOT EXCHANGE THEIR TOXINS; HOWEVER, THEY CAN ABSORB SUBSTANCES FROM THE SOIL THAT ARE DANGEROUS FOR HUMANS.

CHAPTER 2

HOW MUSHROOMS ARE "BORN"

The lifespan of mushrooms varies greatly based on the species but, in general, it follows a series of phases that start with the germination of a microscopic spore.

Let's find out how the spores – invisible to the naked eye – develop mycelium and create the largest living being on Planet Earth!

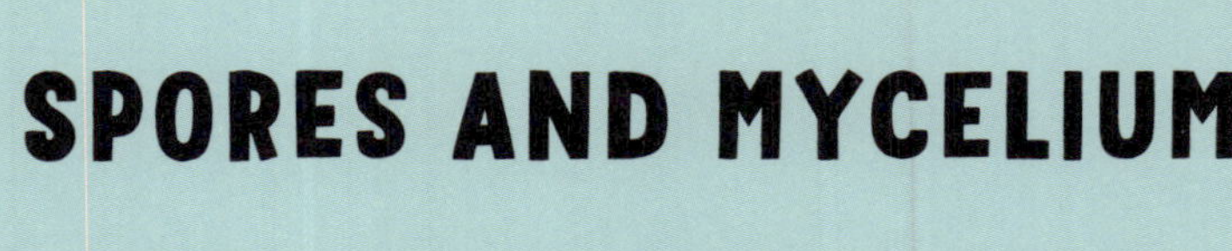

SPORES AND MYCELIUM

Spores are the *reproductive cells* of mushrooms, and are produced by and released from the **hymenophore**, which is the part under the cap.

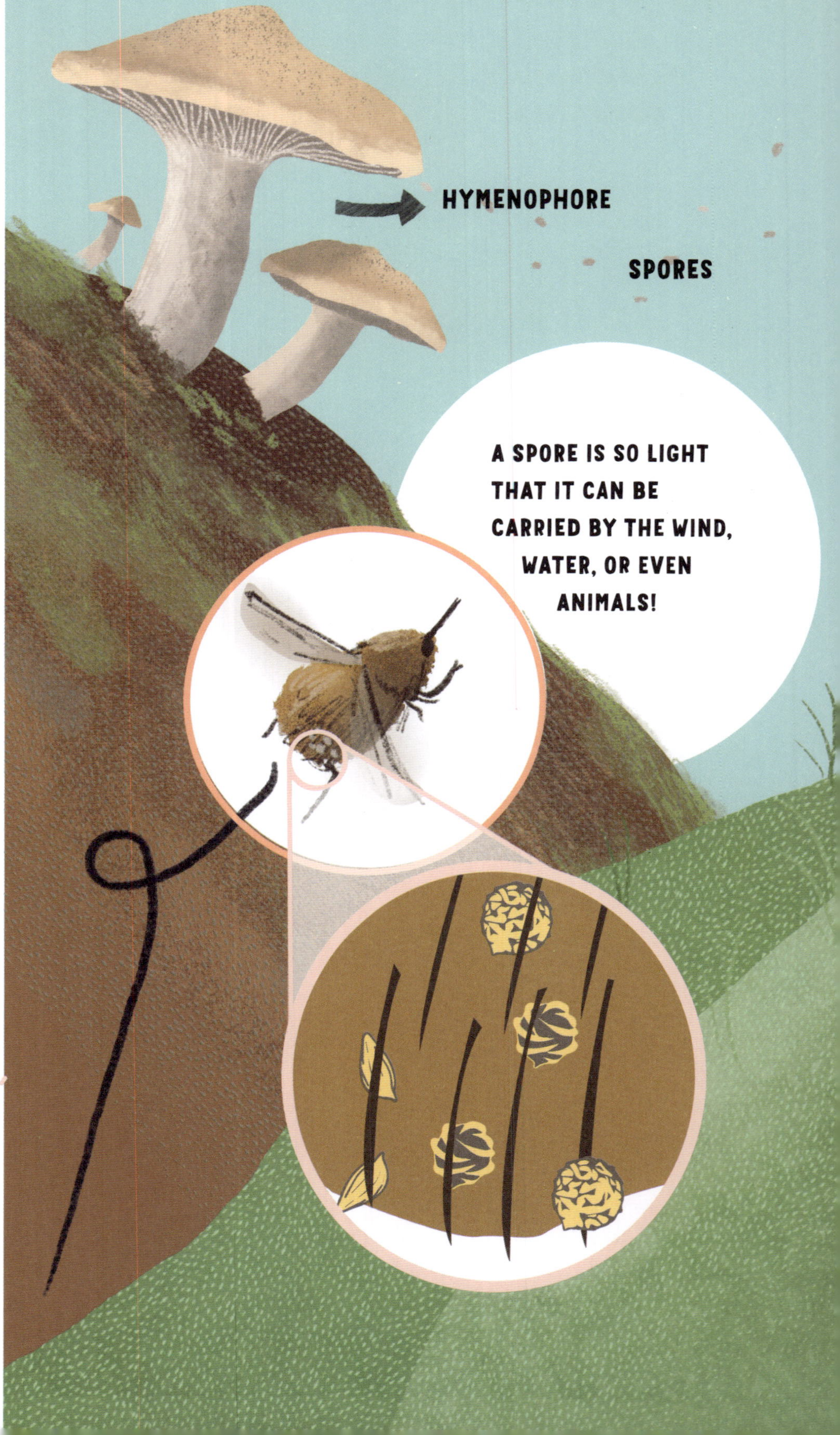

HYMENOPHORE

SPORES

A SPORE IS SO LIGHT THAT IT CAN BE CARRIED BY THE WIND, WATER, OR EVEN ANIMALS!

A mushroom is born following the *germination* of one **spore** landing in a good environment: from here, the cells multiply and connect to form long strands, the **hyphae**, which slowly become a real tangle of lots of connections: the **mycelium**.

IT HAS NO HANDS TO GRAB; IT HAS NO LEGS TO MOVE; IT DOESN'T HAVE A HEAD; IT HAS NO EYES, NOSE, MOUTH, OR EARS: THE MYCELIUM IS ALL OF THESE THINGS PUT TOGETHER!

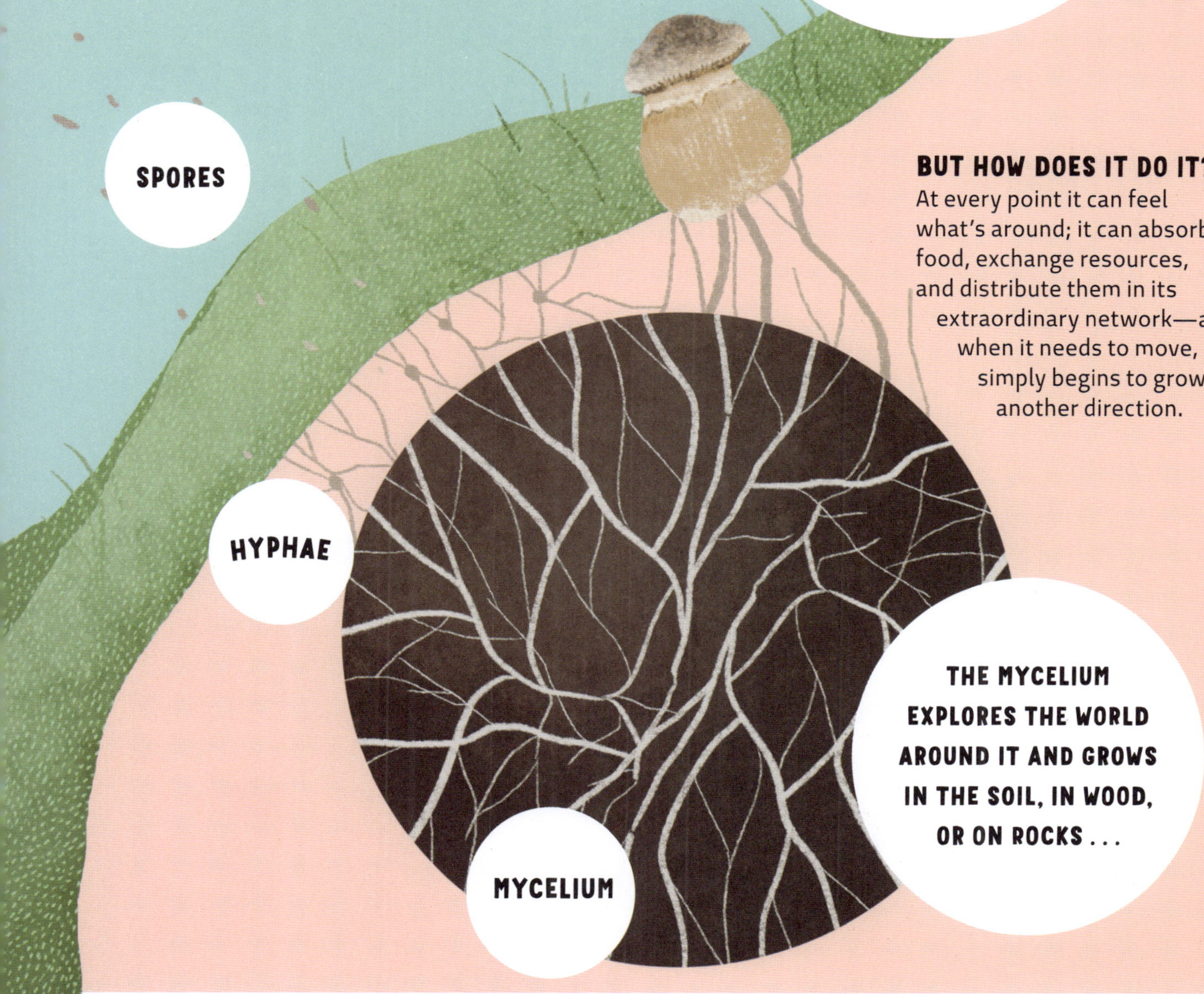

SPORES

BUT HOW DOES IT DO IT?

At every point it can feel what's around; it can absorb food, exchange resources, and distribute them in its extraordinary network—and when it needs to move, it simply begins to grow in another direction.

HYPHAE

THE MYCELIUM EXPLORES THE WORLD AROUND IT AND GROWS IN THE SOIL, IN WOOD, OR ON ROCKS . . .

MYCELIUM

REPRODUCTIVE CELLS: these are the cells that, by meeting and joining together, allow the formation of new life.

GERMINATION: the process by which a spore begins to form new hyphae and mycelium.

SPOROPHORES AND SPORES

AT FIRST THE MYCELIA GROWS AND EXPLORES THE SURROUNDING ENVIRONMENT.

When the mycelia of two different mushrooms meet, many things can happen . . .

If the two mushrooms belong to different species, they may reject each other, exchange resources or attack each other with various chemical substances.

If the two mushrooms belong to the same species and are compatible, a new mycelium is formed that will grow and create sporophores: the mushroom's "fruits".

Sporophores are essential for the production and release of the spores that will guarantee the mushroom's chance to reproduce and scatter itself far and wide.

EACH FULLY GROWN SPOROPHORE CAN PRODUCE BILLIONS AND BILLIONS OF SPORES! THEY ARE INVISIBLE TO THE NAKED EYE BUT WHEN THEY ALL COLLECT IN ONE PLACE. THEY LOOK LIKE A VERY FINE POWDER IN A VARIETY OF COLORS: CREAMY-WHITE, REDDISH-BROWN, PINK, DARK BROWN, OR BLACK.

THE JOURNEY OF A SPORE

A SPORE IS 500 TIMES SMALLER THAN A GRAIN OF SAND!

WHEN THE SPORE IS READY IT DETACHES ITSELF FROM THE BASIDIUM, IT STARTS TO FALL DOWNWARD BUT IT IS UNLIKELY TO REACH THE GROUND: AS SOON AS IT LEAVES, IT IS CAPTURED BY AIR CURRENTS THAT ARE INVISIBLE TO US.

BILLIONS OF SPORES ARE PROJECTED AND SCATTERED INTO THE AIR, BUT ONLY A FEW WILL FIND THE RIGHT CONDITIONS TO GERMINATE.

THESE CURRENTS ARE STRONG ENOUGH TO MOVE THE SPORES, LIFTING THEM INTO THE AIR AND ALLOWING THEM TO BE TRANSPORTED FAR AWAY FROM THE MUSHROOM THAT PRODUCED THEM.

NOW THE CYCLE CAN BEGIN AGAIN: NEW MYCELIUM IS READY TO BE SPREAD OVER THE GROUND, WHERE IT WILL GROW AND ESTABLISH MANY EXTRAORDINARY RELATIONSHIPS!

NOW IT'S TIME FOR AN EXPERIMENT!

WHAT YOU WILL NEED:

- a fresh mushroom (it can be shop-bought!)
- a sheet of white paper
- a transparent container

REMEMBER TO ASK AN ADULT FOR HELP.

METHOD:

1 Separate the cap from the stalk. Place the cap on a sheet of white paper, with its hymenophore facing upwards.

2 Cover the cap with a transparent container (for example, a glass). This way you will keep your mushroom damp and stop the spores scattering in the air.

3 Wait at least 12 hours.

4 Remove the glass and pick up the cap: now you can see the incredible imprint created by the spores of your mushroom!

IF YOUR MUSHROOM'S IMPRINT ISN'T VERY CLEAR, IT COULD BE BECAUSE THE SPORES ARE WHITE OR CREAM. YOU CAN TRY AGAIN USING A SHEET OF BLACK PAPER!

EXTRAVAGANT DISPERSION

There are mushrooms that rely on the rain or other animals to scatter their spores far and wide!

Pilobolus sp.

Some mushrooms are real spore-throwing champions! These microscopic mushrooms that grow on the poo of herbivores cause the pressure of the liquid inside them to increase so much that, at a certain point . . .

THE SPORES GET THROWN OUT AT VERY HIGH SPEED!

CANNON MUSHROOMS

Cyathus sp./Crucibulum sp.

They almost look like small eggs inside birds' nests, but instead they are single structures, each containing millions of spores . . .

IT TAKES JUST ONE DROP OF RAIN TO HIT THE MUSHROOM AND RELEASE THEM.

SPLASH EFFECT

Bovista sp.

THESE BALLS PEEKING BETWEEN THE BLADES OF GRASS USE THEIR SHAPE TO MOVE FAR!

Once ready, the sporophores of these mushrooms detach themselves from the ground and roll like marbles. Carried by the wind, they break and release millions of spores.

ROLL!

Phallus impudicus

Their rotten smell attracts many insects that, unable to resist, end up landing on them.

FOR EXAMPLE, FLIES GET COVERED IN SPORES AS THEY FEED ON THE MUSHROOMS. WHEN THEY FLY AWAY, THEY CARRY THE SPORES, SPREADING THEM EVERYWHERE THEY LAND.

Lycoperdon sp.

These round mushrooms patiently await a few drops of rain, a gust of wind, or an animal to make contact and make them puff.

EACH FULLY GROWN MUSHROOM HAS A HOLE ON ITS SURFACE WHICH RELEASES A COLORFUL CLOUD MADE OF MILLIONS OF SPORES THAT THE BREEZE THEN CARRIES AWAY!

Hypogean mushrooms

How do mushrooms that produce underground sporophores, such as truffles, spread their spores? They count on animals! Wild boars, deer, rodents: many are able to detect these treasures hidden underground thanks to a much more developed sense of smell than ours.

AFTER FINDING AND EATING THEM, ANIMALS SPREAD THE SPORES THROUGH THEIR POO.

IRRESISTIBLE SMELLS

LIFESTYLES AND NUTRITION

Mushrooms have different lifestyles and, depending on their characteristics, they can be called: SAPROPHYTES, when they feed on the remains of dead organisms; PARASITIC SYMBIOTES, when they get food from living organisms; and MUTUALIST SYMBIOTES, when they form alliances with other organisms, swapping resources or "favors" with them.

SAPROPHYTIC MUSHROOMS

They play an essential role on our planet: they are **decomposers**. Thanks to them, complex matter that is inedible for most living beings (for example, wood) is transformed into food for many other organisms, including us.

THIS IS THE LIFESTYLE OF MOST MUSHROOMS.

PARASITIC SYMBIOTIC MUSHROOMS

They feed on living organisms, passing on diseases which sometimes lead to **death**. Parasitic mushrooms exist for **plants**, **animals**, and even **other mushrooms**.

PREDATORY MUSHROOMS

They are microscopic mushrooms that feed on the tiny animals in soil. Thanks to their noose-shaped hyphae, they are able to **capture prey**, such as microscopic worms.

EACH MUSHROOM HAS ITS OWN CHARACTERISTIC LIFESTYLE, BUT THAT CAN CHANGE.

THIS IS THE CASE OF SOME MUSHROOMS WHICH, AFTER LIVING AS PARASITES ON LIVE ORGANISMS (SUCH AS PLANTS) CAUSE THEIR DEATH AND THEN CONSUME THEM; THEY CHANGE TO A SAPROPHYTIC LIFESTYLE.

MUTUALIST SYMBIOTIC MUSHROOMS

They live in close **alliance** with other organisms and help each other to survive, grow, or reproduce. They get part of their food by **collaborating** with the organism with which they are in symbiosis.

There are mushrooms that form this type of bond with **plants** or with **bacteria**; others with **animals,** and some even with **other mushrooms**!

COMMUNICATION IN MUSHROOMS

You will never see two mushrooms talking or waving to each other, yet the mushroom mycelium is constantly busy communicating!

A LANGUAGE YET TO BE DECODED
Mushrooms use a very complex language that is very different from ours, so we haven't decoded it yet.

IT IS NOT MADE OF SOUNDS AND WORDS BUT OF CHEMICAL SUBSTANCES AND VERY WEAK ELECTRICAL SIGNALS WHICH ALLOW THE MYCELIUM TO FEEL THE SURROUNDING ENVIRONMENT, ADAPT TO IT, AND INTERACT WITH OTHER ORGANISMS!

PLANTS, ALGAE, BACTERIA, OTHER
MUSHROOMS, AND EVEN ANIMALS:
BY PRODUCING AN INCREDIBLE VARIETY
OF SIGNALS, MUSHROOMS ARE ABLE TO
SEND CLEAR MESSAGES TO ANYTHING
THAT CAN UNDERSTAND THEM, AND
SO END UP INFLUENCING AND
CONNECTING ALL THE LIVING
BEINGS OF THE ECOSYSTEM!
DO YOU WANT
TO KNOW MORE ABOUT THE
INCREDIBLE INTERACTIONS
OF MUSHROOMS AND WHO
THEY COMMUNICATE WITH?
TURN THE PAGE!

CHAPTER 3

RELATIONSHIPS WITH OTHERS

Mushrooms are specialists in forming relationships, swapping, taking, and giving.

They've always been able to communicate and interact with all the living beings they encounter, and their lives are so connected with other plants, animals, and bacteria, that they form a really important part of ecosystems.

WHAT IS SYMBIOSIS?

The term symbiosis means "living together" and describes the curious **coexistence between two different organisms**. These cohabitations are not all the same: there is MUTUALISM, in which both participants benefit; PARASITISM means that one of the creatures live at the expense of the other, harming it; and in COMMENSALISM no one gets hurt.

MUTUALISM: MYCORRHIZAE

Mycorrhizae are a symbiosis between the **mycelium** of some mushrooms and the **roots** of plants. They are very common in nature, but invisible to the naked eye.

BUT HOW DOES IT WORK?

The **mycelium** covers the **roots** of the plant, allowing them to better absorb **water** and **minerals** from the environment; in exchange, the plant provides the mushroom with **sugars**, which it produces during photosynthesis.

ENDOMYCORRHIZAE

When the mycelium of the symbiotic fungus sneaks inside the cells of the plant's roots, it is called **endomycorrhizae** ("endo" means inside). This **mycorrhiza** is present in approximately 80 per cent of terrestrial plants, especially **herbaceous ones**, like wheat, and in vegetables and many other plants—even **wild orchids**!

ALMOST ALL THE WILD ORCHIDS THAT GROW IN OUR WOODS AND MEADOWS ARE ONLY ABLE TO BLOOM THANKS TO THEIR SYMBIOSIS WITH A MUSHROOM!

ECTOMYCORRHIZAE

In this case the **mycelium** of the mushroom forms a coat around the roots without penetrating them. They often involve the **trees typically found in forests**, like oaks, chestnuts, beeches, fir trees, and many others.

LICHENS: ANOTHER TYPE OF MUTUALISM

What are all those tufts, leaves, and colored crusts that decorate the bark of trees and rocks? Although their appearance is varied, they are all **lichens**, the result of an incredible **mutualistic symbiosis** between mushrooms and organisms capable of photosynthesis, such as algae and some bacteria.

Thanks to co-operation, the chances of surviving and prospering are much greater, even in harsh environments!

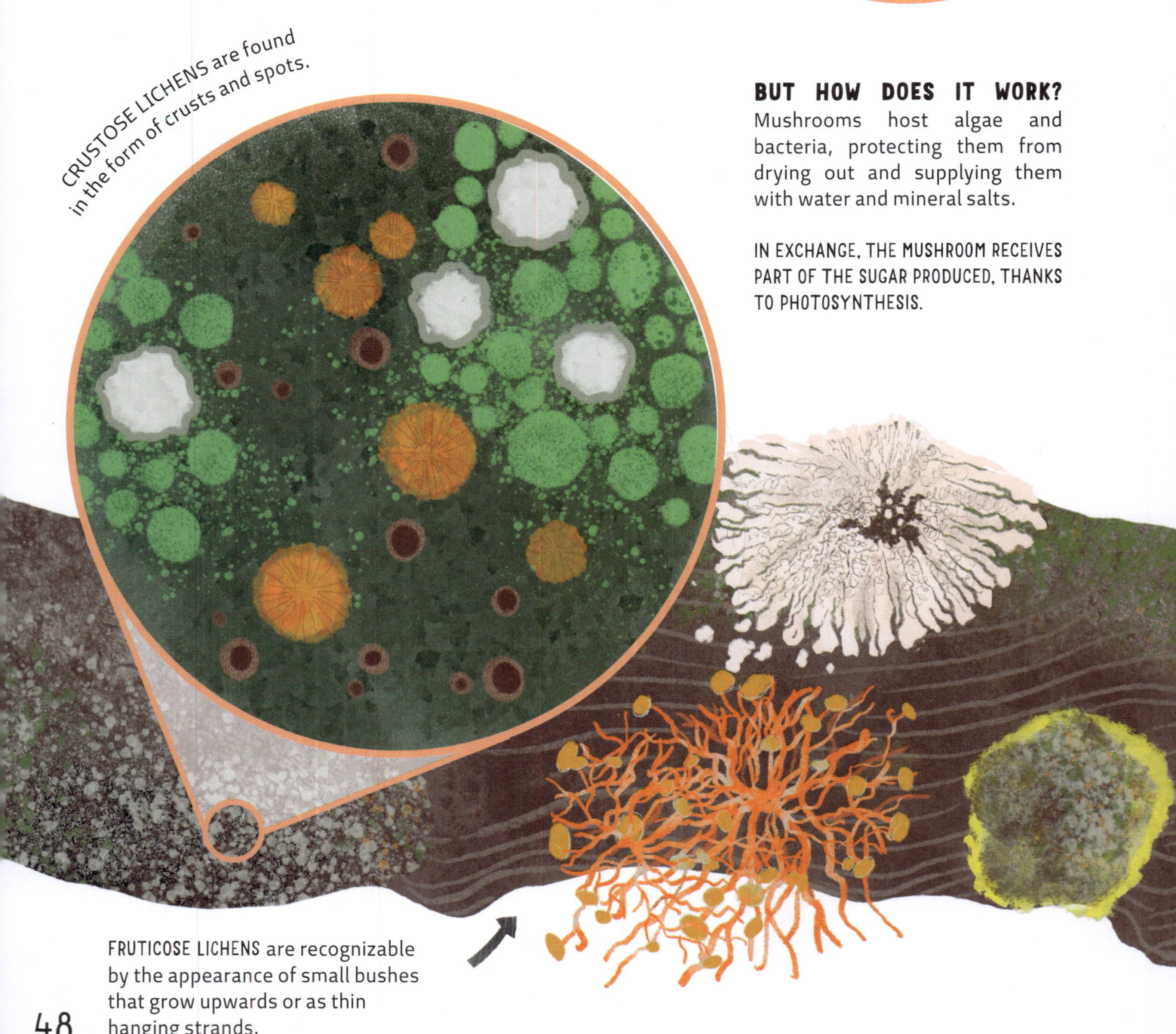

CRUSTOSE LICHENS are found in the form of crusts and spots.

BUT HOW DOES IT WORK? Mushrooms host algae and bacteria, protecting them from drying out and supplying them with water and mineral salts.

IN EXCHANGE, THE MUSHROOM RECEIVES PART OF THE SUGAR PRODUCED, THANKS TO PHOTOSYNTHESIS.

FRUTICOSE LICHENS are recognizable by the appearance of small bushes that grow upwards or as thin hanging strands.

LICHENS AROUND US

Thanks to their exchange with **algae** and **bacteria**, lichens are able to live in all kinds of environments and surfaces, thriving even in what seems like isolated and **unwelcoming corners** of our planet.

LICHENS OFTEN GROW ON WOOD, ROCK, AND SOIL, BUT THEY CAN SPREAD OVER MANY DIFFERENT SURFACES, SUCH AS WALLS, ROOF TILES, METAL PIPES, CARS, PLASTICS, AND MANY OTHER ARTIFICIAL OBJECTS.

THERE ARE A FEW SPECIES OF (VERY RESISTANT) LICHENS WHERE THE AIR IS POLLUTED . . .

LICHENS AS BIOINDICATORS

Observing lichens can give us very important clues about the **health of the environment** around us: we can understand how clean the air is, based on their variety and quantity!

Organisms that, like lichens, are able to give us information on the quality of the environment in which they live are called **bioindicators**.

. . . AND MANY LICHENS OF DIFFERENT SPECIES WHERE THE AIR IS CLEAN.

LICHENS GROW VERY SLOWLY AND CAN LIVE FOR UP TO 300 YEARS!

LEAFY LICHENS are similar to small colorful leaves.

SYMBIOSIS WITH ANTS

In the forests of Central America, there are many ants of different species which are always busy working. They are the **leaf cutter ants**.

The name comes from their behavior: they cut pieces of leaves and take them inside the rooms of their anthill.

THE LEAVES ARE THEN USED AS THE BASE TO GROW A SINGLE MUSHROOM.

THIS MUSHROOM NOW LIVES IN SYMBIOSIS WITH THE ANTS AND NO LONGER PRODUCES A SPOROPHORE!

SO HOW DOES IT MANAGE TO SPREAD? THAT'S ANOTHER TASK FOR THE ANTS!

WHEN THE NEW QUEENS ARE READY TO CREATE THEIR COLONY, THEY BRING WITH THEM A PIECE OF THE MUSHROOM THEY PRODUCE. THEY KEEP IT IN THEIR STOMACH AND, ONCE THEY FIND THE RIGHT PLACE, START TO GROW IT IN THEIR NEW ANTHILL.

BUT HOW DOES IT WORK?

It's an **amazing collaboration** that started millions of years ago, and results in the survival of both living things, which are completely dependent on each other: a perfect example of **obligatory mutualistic symbiosis**!

The ants feed their "mushroom farm" by preparing pieces of leaves, keeping the mycelium clean from mold, fertilizing it (with their own poo!), and spreading it in new rooms of the anthill.

SO THE MUSHROOM THRIVES, THANKS TO THE ANTS, AND PRODUCES UNIQUE STRUCTURES RICH IN NUTRIENTS THAT THE COLONY WILL USE AS FOOD: A REWARD FOR THE ANTS' HARD WORK.

TERMITES ALSO FORM A MUTUALISTIC SYMBIOSIS WITH A MUSHROOM, WHICH GETS LOOKED AFTER BY THE COLONY, AND IS ABLE TO PRODUCE SPOROPHORES THAT WEIGH UP TO 4 POUNDS!

PLANT-PARASITIC MUSHROOMS

Shelves on the trunks, small balls on the leaves, crusts, and dusts of all colors: these **mushrooms** really have some **incredible** qualities, and they are not always easy to spot!

Ganoderma applanatum

They look like shelves, but they are mushrooms and a **nightmare** for many trees. They infest the plant, weakening it and often causing it to die.

THE MYCELIUM STARTS FROM THE ROOTS OR SMALL WOUNDS, AND FROM THERE DEVELOPS, GROWS, AND SPREADS THROUGHOUT ITS HOST.

Exobasidium rhododendri

The pink and yellow balls on the leaves of **rhododendron** may appear to be its fruits. However, it is an infection caused by a **parasitic mushroom** that enters the plant through small wounds on the trunk or roots and produces these **richly colored structures**.

THE MUSHROOM WEAKENS THE RHODODENDRON AND LIMITS ITS GROWTH, TAKING AWAY ITS FOOD WITHOUT KILLING IT.

Hemileia vastatrix

This fungus attacks the **leaves of the coffee plant**, on which it appears as orange, powdery spots.

IT MAY NOT LOOK PARTICULARLY SCARY BUT, AROUND THE END OF 1800, IT CAUSED THE TOTAL DESTRUCTION OF THE VERY IMPORTANT COFFEE PLANTS ON THE ISLAND OF CEYLON, NOW KNOWN AS SRI LANKA.

INSECT-PARASITIC MUSHROOMS

The lifestyle of these mushrooms is so **unsettling** that it inspired stories, books, films, and video games about **zombies**! Don't worry, though, they are not interested in us humans! Their life begins as a microscopic spore that ends up on the body of an insect: it will germinate on it and then infect its insides with its own **mycelium**.

BUT HOW DOES IT WORK?

As it grows, the mushroom controls the behaviour of its unfortunate host by pushing them to **perform unusual actions** until the insect climbs to a position high above the ground, and dies.

BY THEN THE MUSHROOM IS FULLY GROWN AND PRODUCING THE STRANGEST-LOOKING SPOROPHORES. THE DEAD INSECT WILL REMAIN FIRMLY IN THE PERFECT POSITION FOR THE SCATTERING OF THE MUSHROOM SPORES.

THERE ARE DIFFERENT SPECIES OF INSECT-PARASITIC MUSHROOMS AND EACH OF THEM USUALLY TARGETS VERY SPECIFIC FAMILIES AND GROUPS. FLIES, ANTS, BEDBUGS, BUTTERFLIES, AND EVEN SPIDERS CAN BE ATTACKED BY THESE DEADLY ORGANISMS!

SO, ARE MUSHROOMS GOOD OR BAD?

There are many **parasitic mushrooms**; they might seem small, insignificant, and nasty for their scary behaviors. However, we shouldn't be too quick to judge: they are so **widespread** and numerous that they can **really influence the environment**.

THEY HAVE CAUSED FAMINE, DISEASES, AND EXTINCTIONS, BUT IT IS ALSO THANKS TO THEM THAT LIFE ON THE PLANET AS WE KNOW IT TODAY IS POSSIBLE.

Let's find out more in the next chapter!

CHAPTER 4

GOOD OR BAD?

At first glance, any parasitic mushroom may seem "bad", but appearances are often deceiving!

For the victim, the parasite is nasty: it takes everything it needs without giving anything back!

From the ecosystem's point of view, however, these mushrooms perform very important tasks: they usually strike weak and sick organisms and keep the rest healthy.

VITAL!

Depending on your perspective, parasitic mushrooms can be both good and bad—and there's more: we now know that mushrooms are among the main protagonists of life on our planet, even capable of influencing the fate of entire ecosystems.

THANKS TO THE NETWORKS FORMED BY THEIR MYCELIUM, THEY CAN ABSORB, MOVE, AND EXCHANGE HUGE QUANTITIES OF SUBSTANCES FROM THE ENVIRONMENT.

ONLY A FEW ORGANISMS ARE ABLE TO DECOMPOSE, TRANSFORM, AND RECYCLE SO MANY IMPORTANT SUBSTANCES, WHICH WOULD OTHERWISE BE UNUSABLE. BY DOING THIS, MUSHROOMS PROMOTE THE *BIODIVERSITY* OF MANY OTHER LIVING BEINGS.

THAT'S WHY VITAL IS THE RIGHT WORD TO USE TO DESCRIBE THEM!

BIODIVERSITY: the diversity of life forms; it's higher when there are more organisms of a variety of species. On the other hand, when it is low, there may actually be many organisms, but belonging to just a few species. The more biodiversity, the better!

INVALUABLE HELP FOR HUMANITY

As well as being delicious to eat, mushrooms have led to incredible discoveries, inventions, and revolutions.

THE ICEMAN AND HIS MUSHROOMS

The Similaun mummy was found in 1991; this ancestor of ours is commonly called **Ötzi** and lived more than 5,000 years ago. His body was preserved in the glacier of the **Similaun in Trentino-Alto Adige** (a region in the north-east of Italy) and, in addition to various objects and tools, the experts noticed that he carried with him **two different wood mushrooms**.

WHAT COULD THEY HAVE BEEN USED FOR?

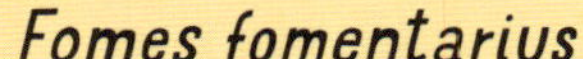

Fomes fomentarius

Called the "tinder mushroom", once dried and crushed it was used to easily light a fire.

FOR MILLENNIA, OUR HISTORY HAS BEEN INTERTWINED WITH THAT OF MUSHROOMS AND, ACTUALLY, THAT IS NOT SO DIFFERENT FROM THE MUTUALIST SYMBIOSIS WE TALKED ABOUT EARLIER.

Fomitopsis betulina

This mushroom had many jobs: it was used to light fires, to sharpen blades, and for its healing properties, which continue to attract the attention of experts.

BAKER MUSHROOMS AND BOTTLED MUSHROOMS

Bread, pizza, wine, and beer would not exist without the fungus we commonly call **yeast**!

EVERYTHING THAT RISES OR FERMENTS DOES SO THANKS TO THESE PARTICULAR MUSHROOMS WHICH ARE ABLE TO TRANSFORM SUGAR INTO ETHANOL AND CARBON DIOXIDE. YEAST MAKES BREAD DOUGH RISE, AND DRINKS BECOME ALCOHOLIC AND FIZZY.

OUR ANCESTORS PRODUCED WINE AND BEER AS EARLY AS 10,000 YEARS AGO, AND LEFT TRACES OF RISEN BREAD MORE THAN 5,000 YEARS AGO!

Saccharomyces cerevisiae

This is the best-known species of yeast: we call it brewer's yeast.

A HELPING HAND IN MEDICINE: PENICILLIN

Let's jump forward to 1928: Alexander Fleming discovered a substance inside a mushroom *(Penicillium)* that would change the history of humanity: **penicillin**.

IT WAS THE FIRST ANTIBIOTIC TO BE DISCOVERED AND IT ALLOWED US TO FIGHT DANGEROUS BACTERIAL INFECTIONS THAT, AT THE TIME, WERE OFTEN DEADLY.

JUST THINK . . . BEFORE THE USE OF PENICILLIN, HUMAN LIFE EXPECTANCY WAS ABOUT 50 YEARS—A FEW YEARS AFTER IT WAS DISCOVERED, THAT JUMPED TO 80. WHAT A HUGE DIFFERENCE!

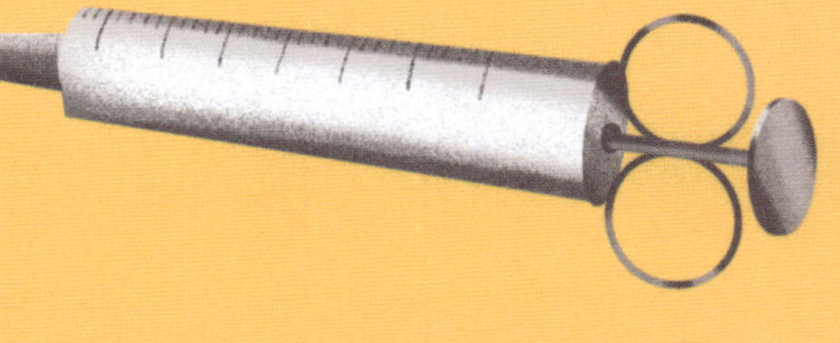

ANOTHER HELPING HAND IN MEDICINE: CYCLOSPORINE

Another substance that has contributed to the great progress made in medicine is **cyclosporine**.

OBTAINED FOR THE FIRST TIME IN 1973 FROM THE MUSHROOM *TOLYPOCLADIUM INFLATUM*, IT HAS HELPED ENORMOUSLY IN THE GROWING SUCCESS IN ORGAN TRANSPLANT.

AN ALLIANCE TO HOLD ON TO!

Following the latest scientific discoveries, mushrooms are proving to be **fantastic allies** that can help us solve some of the most urgent problems of our time.

NEW MYCELIUM-BASED MATERIALS ARE HELPING US TO REDUCE THE USE OF PLASTIC AND ITS BY-PRODUCTS, AND PERHAPS, IN A FEW YEARS, WE'LL SEE THE FIRST BOXES AND PACKAGES MADE OF TOTALLY BIODEGRADABLE MYCELIUM!

DIDN'T WE SAY THAT MUSHROOMS ARE CHAMPIONS AT TRANSFORMING SUBSTANCES? WILL WE EVER BE ABLE TO MAKE THE MOST OF THIS ABILITY TO SOLVE THE PROBLEM OF POLLUTION? WELL, YES!

THE POLLUTION SOLUTION?

Scientists are studying different systems which, thanks to the ability of mushrooms to **absorb and recycle substances**, could help us get rid of many **harmful products** that humans create but struggle to manage.

PLASTIC, OIL, HEAVY METALS, AND PESTICIDES ARE DANGEROUS SUBSTANCES FOR US AND FOR THE ENVIRONMENT: ANY NEW ALLIANCES WE MAKE WITH MUSHROOMS WILL HELP TO DEVELOP SOLUTIONS THAT SOLVE THE PROBLEM OF POLLUTION – AND THAT'S ONLY THE BEGINNING!

CHAPTER 5

ARE MUSHROOMS IN DANGER?

In the pages of this book, we have discovered how the mushroom kingdom is strong and ready to stand up to problems: they were there when the Earth was still desolate, and they have witnessed catastrophes and extinctions of all kinds.

However, the survival of many mushrooms is threatened today by the activities of us humans.

THE IMPORTANCE OF SOIL

Soil is vital for many mushrooms because it is the environment in which **mycelium** develops: it is important that it is **wet enough** and that it does not dry out; it also needs to be rich in nutrients and free of harmful substances.

THE WORST DANGERS!

Uncontrolled agriculture, **pollution**, and **global warming** weaken the soil, making it dry and unsuitable for any life except the most resistant mushrooms.

UNCONTROLLED AGRICULTURE: a method of farming that exploits natural resources without worrying about the negative effects.

GLOBAL WARMING: the increase in temperatures on our planet. Though it doesn't sound like a lot, even just a few degrees of difference can upset the delicate balance of Earth.

MUSHROOMS: DO NOT DISTURB

We have explored the **mysterious** and mostly **invisible kingdom** which grows and stretches beneath our feet, and only occasionally, shows us its "fruits". Much of this world is unexplored and you could be the one who discovers new aspects of these incredible life forms!
How? By learning to look out for them, observe them, and respect them–just like a mycologist!

THE MYCOLOGIST'S KIT:

- **KNIFE** to cut mushrooms, and look at their parts and possible changes in color
- **MAGNIFYING GLASS** and **FIELD MICROSCOPE** to be able to have a closer look
- **CHEMICAL REAGENTS** to determine the species: when in contact with mushrooms, these substances can change color
- **MIRROR** to observe the hymenophore without picking the mushroom
- **TWEEZERS** to take small samples for analysis in the lab
- **CONTAINERS** to store the samples to be analyzed

Since the lives of plants, animals, and mushrooms are so connected, any damage suffered by one of them risks having an impact on the others. Protecting mushrooms therefore means protecting all life on our planet, including our own.

ILLUSTRATORS

ESTER CASTELNUOVO

She studied scenography at the Brera Academy of Fine Arts, in Milan. In addition to collaborating in the editorial field with various publishing houses, she also creates animated scenography and illustrated backdrops for important theatres, such as the Piccolo Teatro in Milan.

VALENTINA FIGUS

She was born in Milan in 1986. She graduated from the Polytechnic in Milan in Communication and Visual Design. She collaborates as a freelancer with various publishing houses, creating interactive digital books, graphic layouts, illustrations, and infographics for educational books.

AUTHORS

GINEVRA PICOCO

A mycologist who has always been fascinated by natural sciences, in particular by the mysterious kingdom of mushrooms.

LORENZO COCCHI

He graduated in Biodiversity and Evolution and now works as a guide and environmental educator in the parks and protected areas of the province of Bologna.

First published in the United States in 2025 by Hodder and Stoughton Limited
First published in Italy by White Star S.r.l.

ISBN: 978-1-804-53873-9
10 9 8 7 6 5 4 3 2 1

Printed in China

Welbeck Children's Books
An imprint of Hachette Children's Group
Part of Hodder and Stoughton Limited
Carmelite House, 50 Victoria Embankment
London EC4Y 0DZ